# Mary Lou Retton

## *America's Sweetheart*

**A Children's Biography by**
*Christine Dzidrums*

*GymnStars Volume 5*

CREATIVE MEDIA, INC.
PO Box 6270
Whittier, California 90609-6270
United States of America

www.CreativeMedia.net

Cover and Book design by Joseph Dzidrums
Artwork by Lyle Lopez

First Edition: March 2014

Library of Congress Control Number: On file

ISBN 978-1-938438-38-7                    10  9  8  7  6  5  4  3  2  1

# Mary Lou Retton

## America's Sweetheart

A Children's Biography by
*Christine Dzidrums*

**GymnStars Volume 5**

*For Ashley*

# Table of Contents

*"I think that any parent should try their child out at gymnastics."*

## Chapter One

# *A Young Gymnast*

On January 24, 1968, a young couple beamed with pride as they cradled their newborn daughter in their loving arms. Ronnie and Lois Retton named their precious baby: Mary Lou. Although the infant was merely a few hours old, she quickly captured her parents' hearts. As fate would have it, sixteen years later, America would also fall in love with their daughter.

Ronnie and Lois raised their five children in Fairmont, West Virginia. A neighborly town whose name is short for "Fair Mountain," Fairmont attracted many young couples looking to raise their budding families in a serene environment. Not surprisingly, the town's nickname was "Friendly City."

Mary Lou Retton grew up as the youngest child. She had three older brothers, Ronnie, Donnie, Jerry, and a big sister named Shari. Although Mary Lou had protective siblings, she was a fiercely independent girl who never needed much defending at all!

Despite being a tiny child, Mary Lou was absolutely fearless. The unapologetic tomboy, with the Dutch-boy haircut and big brown eyes, boasted a hearty laugh, booming confidence and a bubbly personality.

Thankfully, the large family lived in a rambling house on a spacious lot. When the robust Retton siblings were not running around their sizable backyard, they made use of the family swimming pool. During West Virginia's icy winter months, the children spent much of their free time playing in the family game room.

A rambunctious youth, Mary Lou displayed so much energy that her mother often scrambled to keep the small tot busy and happy. Eventually, the youngest Retton landed in dance classes at a local studio. The talented girl loved exploring many different dance genres, including tap dance and ballet. Most of all, she excelled at acrobatics, a style that stresses balance, sprightliness and coordination.

Outside the dance studio, Mary Lou often tumbled for hours in her backyard. She mastered somersaults, cartwheels and backflips. The nimble child took great satisfaction in practicing a skill over and over again until she could perform it perfectly.

Shortly after Mary Lou's fifth birthday, she began a gymnastics class at West Virginia University. The gifted gymnast enjoyed practicing on the sport's four events: floor exercise, balance beam, uneven bars and vault. She especially adored tumbling across the springy mat during floor exercises and flying through the air while performing a vault. The petite youngster with short, muscular legs swiftly developed into a powerful athlete with dynamic, thrilling gymnastics moves.

Mary Lou's athletic talent did not surprise anyone who knew the Rettons. After all, the girl's father had played football in college. Even more impressively, he was also a professional baseball player for many years. The talented shortstop reached as high as the New York Yankees Class AA team before ending his career.

Mary Lou loved gymnastics more than anything. The eager student always studied the sport's top gymnasts and mirrored their greatest qualities. She dreamed of one day becoming one of the world's best athletes.

In July of 1976, Mary Lou watched the Montreal Olympics on television every day. Every four years, the Olympics attracts world-wide athletes who compete in various sporting events. Winners receive a gold medal while second and third-place finishers take home silver and bronze, respectively. Summer Olympic sports include: gymnastics, swimming, soccer and track and field.

The eight-year-old watched the 1976 Olympics with great interest. She admired Olga Korbut, a beloved pig-tailed gymnast from the Soviet Union, who won three gold medals at the 1972 Olympics. The technical trailblazer arrived at the Montreal Olympics dreaming of winning additional medals for her already impressive trophy case.

To everyone's surprise, a new gymnastics superstar emerged in Montreal. Guided by coach Bela Karolyi, Romanian teenager Nadia Comaneci stunned the sports world with her perfect technique and cool composure. The petite brunette had a perfect mixture of difficult routines and elegant artistry.

On day one of the women's team competition, Nadia's tremendous uneven bars routine left spectators speechless. The judges rewarded the fourteen-year-old with gymnastics' first perfect score in competition, a 10.0. Her astonishing achievement sent shock waves around the world and instantly made the young girl a household name.

Several days later, Nadia handily cruised to victory in the all-around competition. Widely considered the sport's highest honor, the gymnast who earns the highest point total on all four events wins the esteemed title.

By the end of the Olympics, Nadia had earned a staggering seven 10.0s. In all, the popular athlete snagged three gold medals, the all-around, balance beam and uneven bars. She also won silver in the team event and a bronze medal on the floor exercise.

Like many young gymnasts at the time, Mary Lou found herself inspired by Nadia's groundbreaking performances. The adolescent began dreaming of competing in the Olympics one day. When would she be old enough? The eight-year-old quickly calculated some numbers. In the summer of 1984, she would be 16 years old, the precise age when many female gymnasts hit their competitive peak.

That settled it! In that moment, Mary Lou Retton set the biggest goal of her life. The unknown gymnast from Fairmont, West Virginia, vowed to compete at the 1984 Olympics!

The brazen youngster suddenly turned to her mom, who sat beside her on the couch. Mother and daughter had spent every day watching the Olympics together.

"Mommy, I'm gonna go to the Olympics," Mary Lou proclaimed. "And I'm gonna win!"

*"You can achieve anything you
set your heart to do."*

## Chapter Two

# OLYMPIC DREAMS

In October of 1978, the International Olympic Committee awarded Los Angeles, California, the exclusive rights to host the 1984 Summer Olympics. Americans rejoiced at the news. In particular, many U.S. athletes felt delighted to learn that they might compete at an Olympic Games in their home country.

Over the next few years, Mary Lou continued pursuing her gymnastics career by competing in several meets on the East Coast. The rising star thrived under the pressure of competitive gymnastics. She loved showcasing difficult skills for critical judges and worked hard to improve her scores. The charming youngster also loved performing for large, enthusiastic crowds.

A strong multitasker, Mary Lou juggled a busy gymnastics schedule with other extracurricular activities. For a while, she was a majorette, a rhythmic gymnast who performs a choreo-

graphed routine to music while twirling a baton. The limber youngster was also a junior cheerleader for many years. Not surprisingly, cheerleading often attracts gymnasts due its heavy use of tumbling and dance.

On most school days, the youngest Retton spent recess playing sports with her male classmates. A terrific baseball player, she was a star pitcher and showed remarkable running speed on the base paths. In fact, the natural athlete could easily outrun most boys in her class.

When Mary Lou was twelve years old, she received an invitation to compete at the 1981 Sports Festival. Hosted by the United States, the junior competition replicated the Olympic experience by hosting various competitions over the course of several days. Athletes even lived in dorms so they could experience the atmosphere of an Olympic Village.

When print and television reporters arrived in Syracuse, New York, to cover the event, Mary Lou had to adjust to cameras following her every move! The West Virginia native began the all-around competition strongly by completing a strong vault, a worthy bars routine and a crowd-pleasing floor exercise. At the end of three rounds, she sat in first place.

Unfortunately, Mary Lou's least-favorite event remained: the balance beam! Her body was short and stocky, a problem for an apparatus that favored long-limbed, flexible gymnasts.

Ultimately, Mary Lou struggled on the event and dropped to second place behind Beth Pope. The highly-competitive athlete felt gutted by the result.

Despite the loss, Mary Lou had captured the attention of the gymnastics world. Even years later, the gymnast credited the '81 Sports Festival with putting her name on the map.

"Going in, I was a total unknown," she told the *Chicago Sun-Times*. "No one knew who Mary Lou Retton was, not even in the gymnastics community."

"But I performed well," the gymnast added. "I was on television, and all the print media wrote that we have a new rising superstar in the sport of gymnastics."

When the focused gymnast returned home, she worked harder than ever. Mary Lou added additional hours to each training day and strove to learn harder skills. Due to her hard work, she earned international assignments in Japan, China and South Africa.

Sometimes people worried that Mary Lou's bustling gymnastics schedule would deny her a normal childhood. The adolescent was quick to point out that her travels offered her the unique opportunity to travel the globe. While most children her age were reading about The Great Wall of China, she was walking on it!

When Mary Lou turned fourteen, sports fans regarded her as one of America's best gymnasts. Still, with the Olympics just two years away, the spunky teenager wanted to become the best in the world. There was one coach who could help her achieve her goal: Bela Karolyi.

*"Don't let people put limits on you."*

# *Chapter Three*

# COACH BELA

On January 1, 1983, Mary Lou moved to Houston, Texas, to begin training under Bela Karolyi. Although Ronnie and Lois Retton were sad to watch their daughter leave home, they fully supported her Olympic dream. The motivated gymnast felt thrilled to train under Nadia Comaneci's former coach.

Meanwhile, Bela enjoyed coaching Mary Lou. He admired the teenager's explosive, quick gymnastics. Plus, she was a hard worker, never complained and rarely lost her composure. All those traits would serve her well in competitions.

Not surprisingly, the Retton family struggled to stay afloat financially. Ronnie and Lois were already paying for college tuitions and Mary Lou's gymnastic' expenses. Now, they needed to produce extra money for their youngest child's room and board in Texas!

Bela's newest pupil lived with a family called the Spillers, whose younger daughter Paige also trained with Bela. The warm hosts were gracious to Mary Lou and always treated her like family. The Spillers' kindness helped ease the gymnast's homesickness and self-doubts regarding her big move.

"I get a little weepy sometimes, but I want to reach my peak," Mary Lou once confessed to *People Magazine.* "There will be time for other things later."

The Karolyi gym demanded strict, grueling workouts from their students. Bela and his wife Marta insisted that every gymnast learn new, harder skills all the time. Their workouts lasted longer than other coaches' sessions, too.

"If you miss even one day you notice it," Mary Lou told *The New York Times.* "Monday is our day off. We only have one workout then."

Interestingly enough, the Karolyis coached another great gymnast, Dianne Durham. Truthfully, Mary Lou enjoyed working beside

her rival. The competitors pushed each other to become better gymnasts.

As the months passed, Mary Lou's gymnastics improved greatly. Thanks to Marta's watchful eye, she became more consistent on the balance beam. By working hard with Bela, the teenager improved her flexibility and form on the uneven bars. She also began generating more power on the floor and vault.

At the 1983 American Classic in Colorado Springs, Colorado, Mary Lou was eager to show the many improvements she had made. However, the fifteen-year-old struggled on day one and lingered in seventh place. Incredibly, on the next day, she rallied strongly and pulled up to a first-place finish! The rising gymnast won the all-around gold medal and earned a 10.0 on vault!

Thanks to that impressive victory, USA Gymnastics named Mary Lou as the alternate to their prestigious international competition, the American Cup. The excited athlete traveled to New York for the event. Although she did not expect to compete, she would watch the other competitors carefully and learn from them.

Except when Dianne suffered an injury, Mary Lou promptly replaced her teammate in the lineup and won the competition! Her all-around total set a record for the event's highest score ever. The gymnastics community stood up and took notice of their newest star!

"I was very pleased with my performance," the American Cup champion remarked modestly after the event.

Several months later, Mary Lou flew to Chicago, Illinois, for her first senior nationals. The focused teen felt ready to face the country's top gymnasts. At the historic event, she scored an all-around bronze medal and won silver medals on the uneven bars and vault.

Soon after nationals, Mary Lou and Dianne traveled to Los Angeles for the McDonald's 1983 International Gymnastics Championships. The competition would give gymnasts the terrific opportunity to compete at UCLA's Pauley

Pavilion, the same arena that would host the 1984 Olympic gymnastics events.

Bela's gymnasts easily dominated the esteemed meet. Dianne won the all-around title with strong performances on every event. Mary Lou placed second and snatched three gold medals in the event finals. The girls' phenomenal efforts caused much commotion in the gym world.

"Dianne and Mary Lou had the best optionals I have ever seen," Don Peters, USA Head Women's Coach, raved to *USGF Gymnastics Magazine.*

Unfortunately, Mary Lou suffered a broken wrist a few weeks later. She would not get to compete for a spot on USA's 1983 world team. Although the plucky youngster felt crushed to miss the event, she kept her sights set on the 1984 Olympics.

The fifteen-year-old created fun teenage memories, too. On Halloween night, she and Dianne trick or treated around a Houston neighborhood. Mary Lou dressed as a punk rocker with blue and pink hair while Dianne wore a scary witch costume.

Naturally, many people wondered if America's top two gymnasts could remain friends while also competing against one another. Fortunately, the girls never believed that training together was a problem.

"We are good friends, but there is a feeling that if she can do it, I can do it," Mary Lou told *People Magazine.* "If she does well, then I have to do well too."

In December of 1983, Mary Lou finally had the opportunity to compete against the world's best gymnasts at the Chunichi Cup in Nagoya, Japan. Gritty and fearless, the teenager defeated many top gymnasts to take the all-around title. Mary Lou's coaches eagerly expressed praise for their star pupil.

"This little girl has a lion heart and a strength I always want to see in my athletes," Bela told *Showtime.*

When the clock struck midnight on January, 1, 1984, the Olympic year had begun. As a little girl, Mary Lou watched Olga Korbut and Nadia Comaneci compete on sports' largest platform. In a few months, the dynamo from West Virginia would compete for Olympic gold, just as her heroes had!

At the 1984 U.S. Championships, Mary Lou won the all-around title by almost a full point over Julianne McNamara, who had recently relocated to Texas to train with the Karolyis. The sixteen-year-old also took home gold medals on vault and floor. After years of hard work and sacrifice, Mary Lou Retton had officially earned the title of America's number one gymnast!

Several weeks later, Mary Lou flew to Jacksonville, Florida, for the 1984 Olympic Trials. Focused and well-trained, the plucky teenager soared to a first-place finish to secure a spot on the U.S. Olympic team. At last, Mary Lou had achieved her childhood dream. She was heading to Los Angeles to compete in the 1984 Olympics!

A strong team would join Mary Lou in Los Angeles. Julianne McNamara, Pamela Bileck, Michelle Dusserre, Kathy Johnson and Tracee

Talavera completed the talented U.S. roster. All six women vowed to earn a medal in the team competition.

Of course, Mary Lou wanted to earn personal hardware, as well. Many thought the talented youth could scoop up medals in the floor exercise and vault. Even more impressively, the teen represented the United States' first legitimate opportunity to win the prestigious all-around championship.

Could Mary Lou Retton be America's answer to Nadia Comaneci?

*"I was just this little kid from West Virginia who nobody thought could do it."*

## *Chapter Four*

# *1984*

In July of 1984, Mary Lou arrived in Los Angeles for the Summer Olympics. The sixteen-year-old moved into a dorm room on the campus of USC, a private college in Southern California. When she was not training with Bela at UCLA, the focused competitor ate at the cafeteria with teammate Julianne McNamara. Then she would return to her dorm and read a book until bedtime.

"I am taking the Olympics as I would any other big international meet," Mary Lou told *USGF Magazine*. "We take meets very seriously, and this one is no different."

On July 1, 1984, the women's gymnastics team competition kicked off at Pauley Pavilion. It had been 36 years since the United States had medaled in the women's team event. At the end of day one, the American women seemed ready to end the long drought when they landed firmly in second place!

Two days later, the team competition con-
cluded triumphantly for the United States. Led
by Mary Lou's strong routines, the American
women won the silver medal! It was their highest
finish ever! Meanwhile, Romania took gold and
China won the bronze medal.

The resolute teen turned her attention to
the individual all-around competition next. Her
chances of winning a medal had skyrocketed
after the Russians boycotted the games due to
political reasons. However, if America's top gymnast wanted to win gold, she would have to beat
Ecaterina Szabo, a Romanian dynamo, dubbed
by many as the "next Nadia."

On August 3, 1984, Mary Lou Retton
walked onto the competition floor for the biggest
meet of her life. Besides Ecaterina, the feisty teen
would battle teammate Julianne McNamara and
Romania's Simona Pauca for gymnastics' highest
honor. American Kathy Johnson had also quali-
fied for the all-around.

As Mary Lou waited to begin her first event,
the uneven bars, Ecaterina polished off a perfect beam set that earned her a 10.0. The steady
American did not let her rival's score rattle her,

though. Instead, she delivered a solid uneven bars routine that earned her a 9.85. The mark would keep her in the running for the gold.

Mary Lou would compete next on her least-favorite event, balance beam. As she warmed up, Ecaterina unleashed a gorgeous floor-exercise performance. Such a stunning display might have rattled any other gymnast, but Mary Lou responded with the best beam of her career.

Midway through the competition, the rivals sat neck and neck for the gold medal. Thankfully for Mary Lou, she still had her two best events left. If she nailed them, she would become the first American woman to win the Olympic all-around competition.

After Ecaterina delivered two imperfect vaults, Mary Lou's chance to grasp the gold medal rose steeply. However, she could not afford a single error. The gritty athlete let loose on the floor exercise with powerful, jaw-dropping tumbling and stuck landings. The nearly 10,000 fans in attendance showered her with a standing ovation.

"That was outstanding," Bela beamed with delight. "That's good. That was good. That was

something. Good job. That's a 10. That's got to be a 10."

The panel of judges agreed with Bela. They rewarded the gymnast with a perfect score! Like Nadia, Mary Lou had earned a 10.0 at the Olympics!

Only one event remained: the vault. The excited crowd stomped their feet and chanted Mary Lou's name as she applied chalk to her hands. In the meantime, Ecaterina's strong bars routine earned a 9.0.

Bela quickly calculated the math. If Mary Lou scored a 9.95 on the vault, she would tie the Romanian for the gold medal. Yet if the American garnered a 10.0, she would win the gold medal exclusively. To make history, his star student needed to execute a flawless vault.

"You can do it," Bela told his athlete. "Never better, Mary Lou. Never better!"

Everyone in attendance at Pauley Pavilion, including Ecaterina, watched Mary Lou as she stood at the end of the vault runway and stared down the horse. The powerful gymnast had completed so many flawless vaults in practice over the years. Now she needed to perform one more perfect vault with the world watching her.

Mary Lou saluted the judges, took a deep breath and sprinted down the runway with all her might. Her body position looked perfect as she sailed powerfully through the air and then stuck the landing! The crowd erupted into excited cheers and chanted 10.0 as the ecstatic American triumphantly clapped her hands. The judges acknowledged the excellent effort with a perfect 10.

When the impeccable mark popped on the scoreboard, Mary Lou exploded into a flurry of emotions. She laughed, pumped her fist and applauded all at once. Bela Karolyi let out a series of whoops as he celebrated his gymnast's victory, just as he had eight years earlier when Nadia had won gold. Meanwhile, the overjoyed audience erupted into celebration.

"I couldn't hold back showing my emotions," the sixteen-year-old later admitted.

A few moments later, Mary Lou performed a second vault. She was perfect again and earned another 10.0. Although vault number two was not necessary, Mary Lou did it anyway. The new

Olympic champion wanted to prove without a doubt that she was the world's best gymnast.

Moments later, Mary Lou stood atop the medal podium glowing with exhilaration. Silver medalist Ecaterina Szabo and third-place finisher Simona Pauca framed the new champion. The arena's sound system played "The Star-Spangled Banner" as organizers raised the American flag.

By the time the Olympics ended, Mary Lou had collected three additional medals. She snagged a second-place finish on vault and bronze medals on the floor exercise and uneven bars. The popular gymnast left Los Angeles with a staggering five Olympic medals.

Thanks to her fireworks athletic display and down-to-earth demeanor, Mary Lou became America's Sweetheart, an adorable girl-next-door who succeeded against all odds. Fans mobbed the superstar on many occasions. Fairmont, Virginia, honored their hometown hero by chris-tening a street in her name. Before she knew it, longtime neighbors and friends were driving on Mary Lou Retton Drive!

Magazines plastered the youth's appealing image on their covers. Sponsors clamored to sign the popular gymnast to promote their products, like M&Ms, workout videos and batteries. She even became the first female athlete to appear on the front of a Wheaties box.

Following the Olympics, Mary Lou visited The White House with the rest of the American Olympic team. She even presented an honorary team jacket to President Ronald Reagan. When the famous athlete tapped the world's most powerful man on his shoulder to get his attention, he gasped in delight.

"Oh my goodness!" President Reagan exclaimed, summoning over his wife, the First Lady. "Nancy, come over here, it's that little Mary Lou we watched!"

Two years after her historic victory, the Olympic champion officially announced her retirement from gymnastics. Soon afterward, she began classes at University of Texas. The freshman studied communications with the hope of becoming a television announcer.

"I think now it's time to pursue my education," the eighteen-year-old announced.

On December 29, 1990, America's Sweetheart married the love of her life, Shannon Kelley, a former quarterback from the University of Texas. The happy couple eventually welcomed four beautiful daughters into the world: Shayla Rae, McKenna Lane, Skyla Brae and Emma Jean.

Years after Mary Lou's inspiring Olympic victory, the icon still touches the hearts of fans everywhere. On the popular video-sharing website, *YouTube*, her historic vaults have netted over one million views. Even today's young gymnasts have cited her as a hero.

In the winter of 1968, when Ronnie and Lois Retton held Mary Lou for the first time, the smitten parents knew their child would change their lives. Little did they know that one day their daughter would touch millions of other people's hearts, too.

Mary Lou Retton would become America's Sweetheart.

# Female Olympic
## All-Around Champions

1952 Maria Gorokhovskaya - Soviet Union

1956 Larisa Latynina - Soviet Union

1960 Larisa Latynina - Soviet Union

1964 Vera Caslavska - Czechoslovakia

1968 Vera Caslavska - Czechoslovakia

1972 Ludmilla Tourischeva - Soviet Union

1976 Nadia Comaneci - Romania

1980 Yelena Davydova - Soviet Union

1984 Mary Lou Retton - United States

1988 Yelena Shushunova - Soviet Union

1992 Tatiana Gutsu - Unified Team

1996 Lilia Podkopayeva - Ukraine

2000 Simona Amanar - Romania

2004 Carly Patterson - United States

2008 Nastia Liukin - United States

2012 Gabrielle Douglas - United States

# *Essential Links*

## Mary Lou Retton's Official Website
*http://marylouretton.com/*

## Mary Lou Retton's Verified Twitter Account
*https://twitter.com/marylouretton*

## Mary Lou Retton Wikipedia Page
*http://en.wikipedia.org/wiki/Mary_Lou_Retton*

## USA Gymnastics Website
*http://usagym.org/*

## United States Olympic Committee
*http://www.teamusa.org/*

## Official Website of the Olympic Movement
*http://www.olympic.org/*

## *About the Author*

**Christine Dzidrums** holds a bachelor's degree in Theater Arts from California State University, Fullerton. She has written biographies on many inspiring women: Joannie Rochette, Yuna Kim, Shawn Johnson, Nastia Liukin, The Fierce Five, Gabby Douglas, Sutton Foster, Kelly Clarkson, Idina Menzel and Missy Franklin.

Christine's first novel, *Cutters Don't Cry*, won a Moonbeam Children's Book Award. She also wrote the tween book *Fair Youth* and the beginning reader books *Future Presidents Club* and the *Princess Dessabelle* series.

Ms. Dzidrums lives in Southern California with her husband, three children and two dogs.

www.ChristineDzidrums.com
@ChristineWriter.

# *Build Your GymnStars™*
## *Collection Today!*

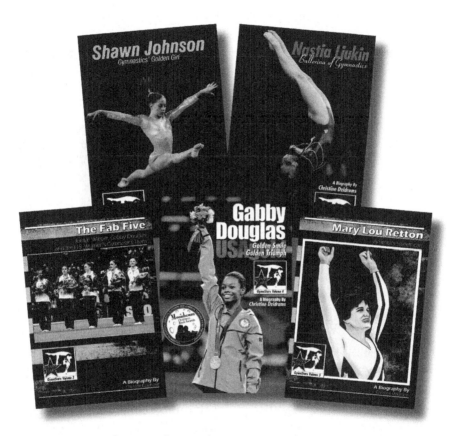

Now sports fans can learn about gymnastics' greatest stars! Americans **Shawn Johnson** and **Nastia Liukin** became the darlings of the 2008 Beijing Olympics when the fearless gymnasts collected 9 medals between them. Four years later at the 2012 London Olympics, America's **Fab Five** claimed gold in the team competition. A few days later, **Gabby Douglas** added another gold medal to her collection when she became the fourth American woman in history to win the Olympic all-around title. The *GymnStars* series reveals these gymnasts' long, arduous path to Olympic glory. *Gabby Douglas: Golden Smile, Golden Triumph* received a **2012 Moonbeam Children's Book Award**.

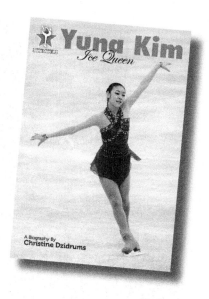

At the 2010 Vancouver Olympics, tragic circumstances thrust **Joannie Rochette** into the spotlight when her mother died two days before the ladies short program. Joannie then captured hearts everywhere by courageously skating two moving programs to win the Olympic bronze medal. *Joannie Rochette: Canadian Ice Princess* profiles the popular figure skater's moving journey.

Meet figure skating's biggest star: **Yuna Kim**. The Korean trailblazer produced two legendary performances at the 2010 Vancouver Olympic Games to win the gold medal. *Yuna Kim: Ice Queen* uncovers the compelling story of how the beloved figure skater overcame poor training conditions, various injuries and numerous other obstacles to become world and Olympic champion.

Our *YNot Girl* series chronicles the lives and careers of the world's most famous role models. *Jennie Finch: Softball Superstar* details the California native's journey from a shy youngster to softball's most famous face. In *Kelly Clarkson: Behind Her Hazel Eyes*, young readers will find inspiration reading about the superstar's rise from a broke waitress with big dreams to becoming one of the recording industry's top musical acts. *Missy Franklin: Swimming Sensation* narrates the Colorado native's transformation from a talented swimming toddler to queen of the pool.

**Ashley Moore** wants to know why there's never been a girl president.

Before long the inspired six-year-old creates a special girls-only club - the **Future Presidents Club**. Meet five enthusiastic young girls who are ready to change the world. *Future Presidents Club: Girls Rule* is the first book in a series about girls making a difference!

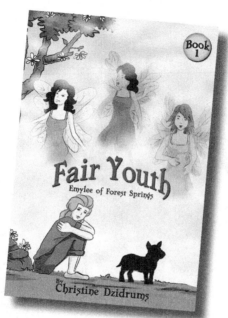

Twelve-year-old Emylee Markette has felt invisible her entire life. Then one fateful afternoon, three beautiful sisters arrive in her sleepy New England town and instantly become the most popular girls at Forest Springs Middle School. To everyone's surprise, the Fay sisters befriend Emylee and welcome her into their close-knit circle. Before long, the shy loner finds herself running with the cool crowd, joining the track team and even becoming friends with her lifelong crush.

Through it all, though, Emylee's weighed down by nagging suspicions. Why were the Fay sisters so anxious to befriend her? How do they know some of her inner thoughts? What do they truly want from her?

When Emylee eventually discovers that her new friends are secretly fairies, she finds her life turned upside down yet again and must make some life-changing decisions.

***Fair Youth: Emylee of Forest Springs*** marks the first volume in an exciting new book series.

Our **YNot Girl** series chronicles the lives and careers of the world's most famous role models. ***Jennie Finch: Softball Superstar*** details the California native's journey from a shy youngster to softball's most famous face. In ***Kelly Clarkson: Behind Her Hazel Eyes***, young readers will find inspiration reading about the superstar's rise from a broke waitress with big dreams to becoming one of the recording industry's top musical acts. ***Missy Franklin: Swimming Sensation*** narrates the Colorado native's transformation from a talented swimming toddler to queen of the pool.

Meet **Princess Dessabelle**, a spoiled, lonely princess with a quick temper.

In *Princess Dessabelle Makes a Friend,* the lonely youngster discovers the meaning of true friendship. *Princess Dessabelle: Tennis Star* finds the pampered girl learning the importance of good sportsmanship.

CPSIA information can be obtained at www.ICGtesting.com
Printed in the USA
BVOW06s1806061115

426096BV00005B/44/P